EXPLORING SCIENCE

# FOOD WEBS

## INTERCONNECTING FOOD CHAINS

### BY SUSAN H. GRAY

Content Adviser: Gary Huxel, Ph.D.,
Department of Biological Sciences, University of Arkansas

Science Adviser: Terrence E. Young Jr., M.Ed., M.L.S.,
Jefferson Parish (Louisiana) Public School System

Reading Adviser: Rosemary G. Palmer, Ph.D., Department of Literacy,
College of Education, Boise State University

Compass Point Books · Minneapolis, Minnesota

Compass Point Books • 3109 West 50th Street, #115 • Minneapolis, MN  55410

Photographs ©: Corbis/Paul A. Souders, cover; PhotoAlto, 4; Shutterstock/Dwight Lyman, 5; Shutterstock/JoLin,
7; Shutterstock/sirano100, 8; Shutterstock/Telnova Olya, 9; Shutterstock/Eric Gevaert, 10; Hans Reinhard/
Photo Researchers, Inc., 11; Shutterstock/Merryl McNaughton, 13; Shutterstock/Thomas E Connelly, 14; Shut-
terstock/jeff gynane, 15; Photo Researchers, Inc./Gary Meszaros, 16; Shutterstock/Pichugin Dmitry, 18; Peter
Arnold/Rauschenbach, F., 20; Photo Researchers, Inc./Gary Meszaros, 21; Shutterstock/Heather Dillon, 22;
Photo Researchers, Inc./Leonard Lee Rue III, 23; Photo Researchers, Inc./Stephen J. Krasemann, 24; Photo
Researchers, Inc./Alexis Rosenfeld, 26; Photo Researchers, Inc./Nigel Cattlin, 27; Shutterstock/Denise Kappa,
28; Photo Researchers, Inc./Christian Gautier, 29; Photo Researchers, Inc./Tom McHugh, 31; Shutterstock/
EcoPrint, 32; Getty Images, 33; Shutterstock/Michael Pettigrew, 34; Shutterstock/Dr. Morley Read, 35; Photo
Researchers, Inc./Gilbert S. Grant, 37; Photo Researchers, Inc./John Mitchell, 38; Shutterstock/David P.
Lewis, 39; Shutterstock/Petr Mašek, 40; Photo Researchers, Inc./ B. MURTON / SOUTHAMPTON OCEAN-
OGRAPHY CENTRE, 42; Photo Researchers, Inc./Fred McConnaughey, 43; Shutterstock/Tina Rencelj, 44;
Shutterstock/Kristin Ondrak, 46.

Editor: Anthony Wacholtz
Designer: The Design Lab
Page Production: Lori Bye
Photo Researcher: Lori Bye
Illustrator: Ashlee Schultz

Art Director: Jaime Martens
Creative Director: Keith Griffin
Editorial Director: Nick Healy
Managing Editor: Catherine Neitge

**Library of Congress Cataloging-in-Publication Data**
Gray, Susan H.
Food webs : interconnecting food chains / by Susan H. Gray ; illustrator,
Ashlee Schultz.
p. cm.—(Exploring science)
Includes index.
ISBN 978-0-7565-3261-1 (library binding)
1. Food chains (Ecology)—Juvenile literature. I. Schultz, Ashlee. II. Title.
III. Series.
QH541.14.G65 2008
577'.16—dc22
2007032680

Visit Compass Point Books on the Internet at *www.compasspointbooks.com*
or e-mail your request to *custserv@compasspointbooks.com*

## About the Author

Susan Gray has a master's degree in zoology, has taught biology,
anatomy, and physiology at the college level, and has worked as a
freshwater biologist. She is now a freelance writer, and has written
more than 70 reference books for young people. Susan especially
enjoys writing books that explore scientific and medical topics. She
also enjoys gardening, playing the piano, and traveling. Susan and
her husband, Michael, live in Cabot, Arkansas.

# TABLE OF CONTENTS

## Chains to Webs

**A TINY YOUNG PLANT** flutters in the breeze. A grasshopper lands next to it, gnaws on the tender shoot, and then hops away. A weasel hears a mouse scrambling across the leaves of the forest floor. The weasel crouches, pauses, and then darts after it, easily catching an evening meal. An eagle soaring high in the sky spots a snake on the ground and dives. The eagle snags the reptile in its sharp talons and carries it off to its young for dinner. A vulture pecks at a week-old heap of small bones, teeth, decaying meat, and bits of hide that was once a rabbit. Maggots crawl over the rabbit as flies hover nearby.

These are all scenes from a food web—the complex network of what eats what within an ecosystem. A community of plants and animals living together, as well as nonliving

An ecosystem is filled with plants and animals that need food to survive.

things such as rocks and air, make up an ecosystem. A food chain is much simpler than a food web. A food chain is a straight line of individual species that eat other individual species. For example, grain is eaten by field mice, and the mice are eaten by hawks.

In reality, things are not that simple. In an ecosystem, grain might be eaten by mice, locusts, chipmunks, and other animals. Mice might be eaten by hawks, snakes, foxes, and other predators. Both a food chain and a food web may include many species within an ecosystem. However, while a food chain follows one single path, a food web is the entire network of interconnected food chains.

After snatching its prey, a hawk carries its meal to a high perch. Holding the animal in its sharp talons, the hawk tears it to shreds and consumes not only the flesh, but the fur and bones as well.

## FOOD WEB VS. FOOD CHAIN

In a **food web**, plants are eaten by many animals, including gazelles, rabbits, and grasshoppers. A rabbit could be eaten by an owl or snake, and so on.

A **food chain** follows a single path. One example of a food chain starts with a plant, which is eaten by a grasshopper. In turn, a fish eats the grasshopper, and a bear eats the fish.

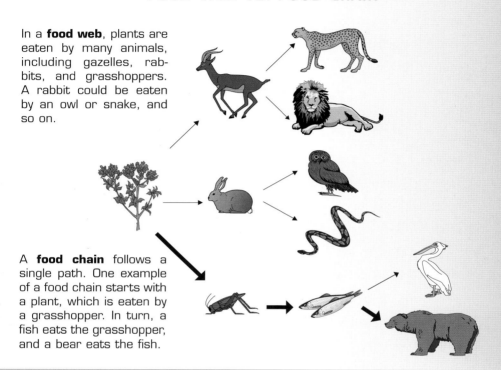

A food web helps us understand the relationships among organisms in an ecosystem. It shows how energy flows through the system from one organism to another. Every organism needs energy to live. Green plants get energy from the sun. Animals get energy from eating plants and other animals. Bacteria get energy from dead plant and animal materials they break down.

The energy flow through a food web is important to plants and animals, but it is also important to human beings. We get our energy from eating other organisms—both plants and animals. We also have the ability to study and alter the effects we have on food webs.

## THE LEVELS OF A FOOD WEB

Every food web starts with organisms that make their own food. In most cases, these are green plants. Their energy comes directly from the sun. They also draw water and nutrients

To collect food, bees gather pollen and nectar, a sweet liquid, from various flowers.

from the soil. Solar energy converts those materials into sugars that keep the plants healthy and help them to grow.

Plants—the organisms at the lowest level of the food
web—are called primary producers. On land, primary producers include mosses, ferns, grasses, shrubs, and trees. In a
lake, primary producers include cattails, duckweed, and tiny
floating plants called phytoplankton. Producers are also called
autotrophs, a word taken from Greek words for "self" and
"food." In other words, producers create food for themselves.

American lotus leaves, which stand on stalks that can be 2 to 3 feet
(60 to 90 centimeters) long, use the sun's energy to produce their own food.

Primary, secondary, and tertiary consumers come next. Because consumers cannot produce their own food as autotrophs do, they are called heterotrophs. The term *heterotroph* comes from Greek words meaning "other food" or "different food."

Primary consumers are animals that feed only on plants. They are also known as herbivores. The term *herbivore* comes from Latin words that mean "plant" and "eater." They are usually small animals, such as insects, mice, and seed-eating birds. Deer, elk, and elephants are three examples of larger plant eaters.

Secondary consumers are animals that feed on herbivores. These include both small insect-eating animals, such as shrews and frogs, and larger animals, such as snakes and weasels.

Squirrels are primary consumers that collect nuts and seeds. Squirrels store excess food in a place that can be easily defended, such as near their nest or under a leaf on the ground.

Tertiary consumers devour the secondary consumers. One example of a tertiary consumer is a cougar that hunts down weasels and snakes. Secondary and tertiary consumers are also called carnivores because they eat other animals. The word *carnivore* is taken from Latin words for "meat" and "eater." Because they track down their prey, they are also known as predators.

The levels of a food web are called trophic levels. The

Many bearded dragons live in habitats where obtaining food only from eating plants can be difficult. To survive, they must eat a combination of plants and a wide variety of insects.

lowest trophic level is always made up of producers. These are usually green plants, but they might also be specialized forms of bacteria.

Some very complex ecosystems might have high levels of consumers. However, systems with more than four trophic levels are fairly rare. Animals at the very highest trophic level are called top predators. These animals have no natural enemies.

The gray wolf is an example of a top predator. With 42 teeth and four fangs, these wolves can consume more than 20 pounds (9 kilograms) of food in a single day.

Nothing hunts them down or preys on them. Large animals such as owls, cougars, and wolves are often the top predators in their food webs.

Not every organism fits neatly into one trophic level. Many animals are omnivores, or "everything eaters" in Latin. They eat a variety of plants and animals. A raccoon, for example, might eat an apple one day, a young squirrel the following day, and a crayfish the next. Therefore, the raccoon serves as a primary, secondary, and tertiary consumer at different times. Human beings also belong in more than one trophic level. A woman beginning her meal with a salad is acting as a primary consumer. When she takes a bite of chicken, she becomes a secondary consumer.

Carnivorous plants are another special case. These plants attract, trap, kill, and digest insects, spiders, and other very small animals. They live in areas where the soil is poor, so they derive some of their nutrients from their unfortunate prey. Plants such as Venus flytraps, sundews, and pitcher plants are unique. They are not only producers, but they are unusual consumers as well.

**DID YOU KNOW?**

There are about 600 species of carnivorous plants.

## DECOMPOSERS—THE CLEANING CREW

Food webs focus our attention on what eats what. However, all organisms die at some point, and then they are no longer an active part of the food web. At this point, they are recycled back into the system. It is the decomposers—mainly bacteria and fungi—that do the recycling.

These organisms break down all kinds of materials—from

Sundews produce a sticky substance on their leaves that appears similar to drops of dew. These plants ingest unsuspecting insects that become stuck on the leaves.

pine needles and tree branches to animal flesh and fur—into basic nutrients that seep into the soil. There they become available to plants.

Decomposers are extremely important but are often overlooked because they are so small. Yet a handful of topsoil might contain billions of these organisms that carry out their work at the microscopic level.

Because they are unable to produce their own food, mushrooms must absorb dead or decaying material from plants, animals, or other fungi.

## Putting Decomposers to Work

Many gardeners enjoy composting, a process that turns piles of grass clippings, leaves, coffee grounds, eggshells, and even cotton rags into a rich, dark material that can improve the soil. This process could not take place without the work of worms, insects, and billions of bacteria.

Composting speeds up the natural decaying process and puts decomposers to work. To compost, gardeners gather lawn clippings and table scraps into heaps. Then they add water to the heaps, stir them, and possibly add dozens of worms to the mix. The worms, along with other decomposers, break the materials down into basic nutrients that growing plants need.

Decomposers, like producers and consumers, release energy as they carry out their normal processes. In compost piles, this energy is converted into heat. It is not unusual for compost heaps to develop temperatures as high as 140 degrees Fahrenheit (60 degrees Celsius).

## CHAPTER TWO

## ⊕ All About Energy

**FOOD WEBS EXIST** wherever there are plants and animals. The plants might be cornstalks, oak trees, or single-celled algae. The animals might be polar bears, blue whales, or small ladybugs. Food webs can be found in oceans, deserts, tropical forests, and even icy Arctic waters. A web might contain a few dozen species, or it might include more than 100. Regardless of how complex a food web is or where it is located, its purpose is to keep energy flowing from one organism to the next.

A starfish obtains food by clamping onto clams or mussels and using its tube feet to suction the two shells apart. The starfish then pushes its stomach through the shells to digest the flesh inside.

No organism can live, grow, and reproduce without energy. Therefore, energy must be available to every organism in an ecosystem. The main source of energy is the sun, and the main users of the sun's energy are green plants.

Solar energy reaches Earth as waves of ultraviolet, visible, and infrared light. Ultraviolet and infrared light waves, which cannot be seen by the human eye, cannot be used by plant cells to make food. Instead, plants trap and use the energy of visible light waves.

Visible light is a combination of red, orange, yellow, green, blue, and violet waves. Colored chemicals inside plant cells absorb these waves. An abundant chemical in green plants called chlorophyll absorbs red, blue, and violet light waves. Other chemicals in the plant absorb yellow and orange light. The green rays, which are not absorbed, are reflected off the plant cells. These rays reach our eyes and make plants appear green.

Plant cells receive light energy from the sun, carbon dioxide from the air, and water from the soil. The cells use the solar energy to convert the carbon dioxide and water into sugar and oxygen in a process called photosynthesis. Oxygen exits the plant through microscopic openings in the leaves and stems. The sugar is then used to sustain the plant. It either goes into building new tissues for growth or is stored for later use.

When an herbivore eats a plant, it takes in the sugars the plant created for itself. The animal takes the plant's energy, and then either uses it for maintenance and growth or stores it. When a carnivore eats the herbivore, the same thing happens. The carnivore takes in the prey's stored energy and either uses it then or stores it for later.

Herbivores such as gorillas get energy by eating various leaves, bark, and fruit.

Even the decomposers are involved in the energy flow. They obtain energy by consuming the remains of plant and animal tissues. They break down this matter and return the nutrients to the soil.

## LOSING ENERGY

As energy moves through the food web, it is neither created nor destroyed, but it may be changed from one form to another. For example, plants convert solar energy into the chemical energy of sugar. But no producer, consumer, or decomposer actually creates new energy or destroys the energy it receives.

Each time energy moves from one trophic level to the next, much of it is lost. Scientists say that, on average, 90 percent of the energy is lost in each transfer. Where does it go?

Not all food that is eaten is processed, broken down, and used for energy. Cellulose is one such food. Cellulose is a complex sugar in the cell walls of plants. Although plants use solar energy to build their cellulose walls, the stored energy is

**DID YOU KNOW?**

Human beings cannot digest cellulose. It passes through the body without providing any energy whatsoever.

useless to the consumer that ingests this material.

There are other things that cause energy losses in a food web. Not all of the available energy moves to the next trophic level. Not every single plant and animal gets eaten. Some simply die, fall to the ground, and are slowly broken down by the decomposers.

Much of the energy is used up before it can go on to the next trophic level. When an organism takes in energy as food, it uses a great deal of it to carry on its life processes, such as breathing, sleeping, and digesting. As it does so, it gives off

In order to get a meal, frogs sit motionless for long periods of time. When an insect wanders nearby, the frog shoots out its tongue, and a sticky substance at the end of the tongue traps the insect.

heat. Carrying on life processes and giving off heat use energy. Until that organism is eaten by another, it uses up energy for itself. It does not pass this energy to the next trophic level.

A food web indicates the flow of energy from one trophic level to the next, but it does not indicate the enormous amount of energy lost in the process. If only 10 percent of the energy flows up to the next level, then a food web with four trophic levels has a tremendous energy loss. The top predator in such a food web receives only 0.1 percent of the energy stored in the plants of the same web.

Because of the energy lost between trophic levels, a largemouth bass that eats a frog only receives 1 percent of the energy stored in the fly the frog consumed.

## Coping With Winter

In most places on Earth, seasons influence plant growth. During warm periods, herbivores have plenty of food because plants grow rapidly and produce fruits, berries, or nuts. As the weather cools, many plants lose their leaves and become dormant. Some herbivores, such as deer or elk, deal with the food shortage by migrating to areas with more food.

Other animals, such as bears and chipmunks, hibernate. Prior to hibernation, animals eat more food than usual. They gain weight and store the added energy as body fat. As the temperature drops, they seek shelter in caves, burrows, or dens, and then fall into the deep sleep of hibernation.

When a food source becomes scarce, elk must travel to another region where the plants are flourishing.

During this period, an animal's breathing diminishes. The heart rate drops, and the body functions slow dramatically. If awakened suddenly, a hibernating animal is groggy and moves about sluggishly. Some hibernators awaken for brief periods during the winter, but others have virtually no activity for months. For example, black bears may rest for up to seven months without eating. When the temperatures warm in the spring, hibernating herbivores awaken just as plants become plentiful once again.

After eating enough food to survive the winter, a chipmunk curls into a tight ball to trap its body heat during hibernation.

## ⊕ Visiting the Pyramids

**IN NATURE, FOOD WEBS** tend to stay in balance. Scientists often refer to a balanced system as being in equilibrium. For a food web to remain in equilibrium, a certain amount of plant material must always be available for plant eaters to survive. Likewise, plenty of herbivores must be available in order for carnivores to survive.

This balanced system is sometimes depicted as a pyramid. Plants are represented by the large base of the pyramid. The smaller layer above represents primary consumers. The next higher layer represents secondary consumers, and so on. Scientists have used the pyramid to represent various ways of looking at a food web. Some use a pyramid of

numbers to indicate there are far higher numbers of plants than of primary consumers. Similarly, there are far higher numbers of primary consumers than of secondary consumers. In nature, however, this is not always the case. In a forest ecosystem, squirrels eat acorns produced by oak trees. Yet the squirrels can easily outnumber the trees.

Therefore, some scientists prefer to use an energy

There must be a balance between the number of lions and zebras for the two species to survive.

pyramid. They use calories to represent the energy available at each trophic level. The greatest amount of energy in any eco-system is stored in its plants. The plants in a food web contain many more calories than the organisms at any other trophic level. The next higher level on the energy pyramid represents the calories available in the bodies of the primary consumers. The next level represents the calories available in the bodies of the secondary consumers, and so on.

## THE ENERGY PYRAMID

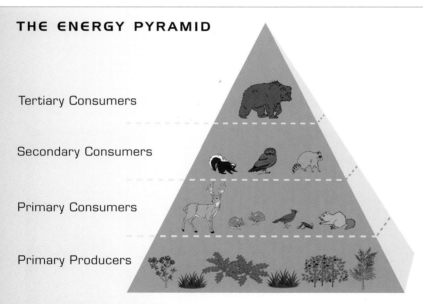

Tertiary Consumers

Secondary Consumers

Primary Consumers

Primary Producers

The greatest amount of energy is in the primary producers at the bottom of the energy pyramid. The least amount of energy is present by the time the energy reaches consumers at the highest level.

Since only about 10 percent of the energy at one trophic level in a food web goes to the next trophic level, an average plant might contain 100 calories, but an average herbivore will only get 10 calories out of it. Each layer's energy will be only one-tenth the amount of the energy in the layer beneath it.

There are some exceptions to the energy pyramid. In certain warm lakes, algae might not seem plentiful enough to feed the many small fish present. An energy pyramid for such a lake indicates that the fish would eventually starve. The algae simply could not provide enough calories to the algae-eating fish. However, the algae grow at an incredibly fast rate in these lakes. In fact, the algae grow as fast as they are eaten.

Because of increased amounts of sunlight between spring and fall, algae reproduce at an extremely fast rate. Ocean water turns a shade of green during this time because of the excess algae.

The availability of sunlight and food also affects the number and variety of producers. In addition, plants need water and good soil. Animals need water, space, and safe places to hide. Clearly, many things can influence the population size at any trophic level.

At times, a particular factor may keep a population from growing. Scientists call this the limiting factor. In a prairie, for example, there may be plenty of sunlight and good soil for plants to survive. However, in an extremely dry year, the shortage of water will cause many plants to wither and die. Water is the factor that limits the plant population.

In certain coral reef ecosystems, disease-causing bacteria might be the limiting factor. The coral animals may have plenty of food and water, but diseases keep their numbers down. This limits the number of animals that feed on the coral. The limiting factor—bacteria—directly limits the coral and indirectly affects organisms in other trophic levels as well.

In northern Tanzania, a maize crop is devastated by a drought, making water the limiting factor.

## Eat Your Veggies

You probably know that eating vegetables is good for you. What you might not know is that it is also energy-efficient. To get 2,000 calories of ham from a pig, a farmer would need a small field of corn equal to 20,000 calories just to feed that one pig. That is because about 90 percent of the energy is lost as it moves to the next trophic level. On the other hand, that same field of corn could provide food for 10 people.

Therefore, in low-income countries, people rely on crops rather than on livestock for food. It is much more energy-efficient and less costly to produce crops than to raise animals.

Because energy is lost between each trophic level, it is more energy-efficient to eat food at the lowest trophic level, such as corn, lettuce, and peas.

## Out of Balance

**WHEN ONE TROPHIC LEVEL** gets out of balance, all other levels are affected. Scientists have seen this occur many times. In some cases, the unbalanced web is caused by a natural event, and in other cases, it is not.

In a lake food web, the producers might be algae, submerged weeds, and lily pads floating on the surface. The algae might be microscopic cells floating freely in the water or strands of cells clinging to underwater stumps. Tiny floating animals called zooplankton feed on the algae. Fish, such as shad, eat zooplankton. Other fish, such as largemouth bass, eat the shad.

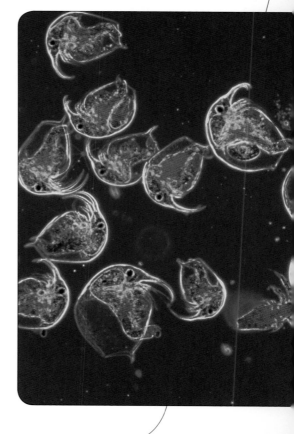

Algae need phosphorus to grow, but most lakes have only a limited amount. In the past, some polluted lakes reached very high levels of phosphorus, and the algae grew out of control. Although it might seem as though it could be good for the herbivores, it was tragic.

Zooplankton, one of the major sources of food for many types of fish, create a back-to-front current that allows them to collect food.

Herbivores could not eat the algae fast enough, and huge masses of algae died. As the algae rotted, the number of decomposers feeding on it skyrocketed. The decomposers used up so much of the lake's oxygen that the zooplankton and fish suffocated and died. Some lakes had "dead zones" where nothing could live. Other lakes could not sustain any life at all.

People eventually became concerned, and the government intervened. New laws were created to limit the amount of pollution in the lakes. As a result, the levels of phosphorus in the lakes decreased, and the food webs returned to normal. The webs regained their state of equilibrium.

## A NATURAL CYCLE

Most food webs have natural ups and downs at the various trophic levels. A good example of this is in the

### DID YOU KNOW?

Top predators help keep the ecosystem in balance. The animals in the trophic level below stay at a steady population, which keeps the population in the next trophic level steady as well. If the top predators changed their eating patterns, it would affect the entire food web.

tundra food web in the cold, northern regions of the world. Lemmings are mouselike creatures that thrive in the tundra. They live in underground burrows during the coldest months of the winter. In the spring, the weather warms and lemmings give birth to their young. At the same time, low-growing plants begin to sprout,

providing them with plenty of food. In some years, the lemming population soars.

This provides a food supply for animals that eat lemmings, such as foxes. With an abundance of food and few enemies, the fox population shoots up. As the number of foxes increase, they begin to use up their own food supply. The lemming population plummets, and soon the fox population does the same. One of these cycles may take several years. It is all part of the equilibrium of the food web.

Scientists believe that lemmings may experience sharp population declines for reasons other than predators, such as disease and harsh weather conditions.

## Magnifying Effects

Some pollutants that make their way into the food web become more concentrated as they move up the trophic levels. This phenomenon, known as biological magnification, has led to warnings about our food supplies.

One such case has to do with mercury in fish. Mercury is known to cause brain damage. Only small amounts of mercury exist naturally in the environment. However, some industries release mercury into the air as a pollutant. This mercury eventually falls or washes into streams, rivers, lakes, and oceans. Fish, clams, and other aquatic animals take the mercury into their bodies.

Many countries protect crabs and other aquatic animals by prohibiting industries from releasing mercury into the environment.

But these animals do not excrete mercury. They retain it in their muscle tissue. When a large fish eats many smaller ones, it ingests the mercury of its prey. Therefore, consumers at the highest trophic levels have the highest concentration of mercury in their tissues.

The biological magnification of mercury has led the U.S. government to issue food warnings. According to the Environmental Protection Agency (EPA), sharks and swordfish have a very high mercury concentration. People, especially children and pregnant women, should avoid eating large amounts of these fish. Cod and catfish exist at lower trophic levels and are much safer to eat.

Although swordfish are considered unsafe to eat by the EPA, some people still fish for them for sport.

## CHAPTER FIVE

## Messing With Mother Nature

**MANY RESEARCHERS TODAY** are striving to understand food webs and the relationships within them. This has not always been the case. In the past, the consequences of tampering with a food web have not been taken into consideration, resulting in disaster. The cane toad of Australia is one example.

Sugarcane is a major crop in Australia that brings in millions of dollars each year. Cane beetles are among the pests that damage or destroy these crops. As primary consumers in the food web, these beetles eat the sugarcane roots, killing or stunting the growth of the plants.

In the 1930s, approximately 100 cane toads were brought in from

Sugarcane stalks can grow to be 30 feet (9 meters) tall. There is a juice inside the stalks that is used to make sugar and molasses.

Hawaii to control the beetles. The toads were supposed to eat the beetles and protect the crops. Some scientists warned that releasing the toads into a new ecosystem could cause grave problems, but the plan was put into action.

The cane toads not only failed to control the beetles, but they also reproduced at a breathtaking rate. They began to compete with other insect eaters for food, and they ate tremendous numbers of bees. Furthermore, the cane toad is highly poisonous. An animal that bites it can suffer a heart attack and die within minutes.

Conservationists in Australia are concerned that several species of small animals that cane toads feed on could become extinct because of the massive number of toads in the area.

The cane toads failed to blend into the food web as secondary consumers. They also killed other members of the web and disrupted natural processes such as the pollination of plants by bees. Because they are poisonous at all stages of life—from egg to tadpole to adult—the toads have no natural enemies. They are still pests in Australia today.

## THE INVADERS

Scientists refer to species that are introduced into a new environment as "invasive species." With no natural enemies, these species can overrun an ecosystem and dramatically alter the food web. Some species, such as piranhas, are unusual pets that people tire of and release into the wild. Others may be exotic plants that homeowners put in their gardens.

Some "invaders" arrive inside ships. Before leaving their overseas ports, ships take on tons of water to help them stay

**DID YOU KNOW?**

Japanese beetles are an invasive species that damages plants and crops in the eastern United States and parts of Canada. The U.S. Department of Agriculture released various types of parasites in an attempt to exterminate the beetles.

balanced. This water, known as ballast, often contains sea-weed, fish, clams, lobsters, and other organisms. When the ships arrive at their destinations, they dump the water. This releases many foreign organisms into the environment. These organisms may have no natural enemies and can disrupt their new food web.

Invasive species have become such a problem that the U.S. government has created the National Invasive Species Information Center. The center provides information about invasive species to help stop their spread. In particular,

Originally from Japan, green fleece algae—also known as dead man's fingers—is an invasive species that has spread all over the world.

lawmakers look to this information to help them formulate laws controlling invasive species.

In the summer of 2007, for example, the U.S. government used the center's information to help create a law making it illegal to import silver carp. The carp are native to Asia and were first used in the United States in the 1970s to control algae in fishponds. However, the carp quickly spread to lakes and rivers and now threaten the food supply of native fish. Thanks to the work of the center, lawmakers, and other government agencies, laws are now in place to keep the carp from spreading into even more waters.

The brown tree snake was accidentally introduced into Guam and is responsible for the extinction of many forest bird species there. The snakes also cause power outages by climbing along and short-circuiting power lines.

## The Great Lakes Invaded

The cane toad problem occurred when people deliberately tried to alter the food web. In the Great Lakes, disruptions to the food web have happened by accident.

In the 1980s, zebra mussels came to the Great Lakes in the ballast of European ships. Before anyone realized it, the mussels were already reproducing rapidly and maturing quickly. The mussels feed by filtering plankton from the water. They devour so much plankton that other organisms cannot get enough to eat. Without sufficient plankton, larval fish die in great numbers. Larger fish that feed on the larvae also die, and people who work in the fishing industry lose their jobs. Clearly, disruption of a food web at one level can have consequences that reach to the other levels.

Scientists have looked at several ways to control the mussels, including chemicals and the introduction of new predators. So far, however, no approach is available that does not have its own consequences.

The large population of zebra mussels continues to be a problem in the Great Lakes today.

# Food Webs Everywhere

**FOOD WEBS EXIST** in almost every environment. In favorable conditions, they are complex, with many species in various trophic levels. In harsh conditions, they are much simpler and involve fewer species.

Tropical regions that are warm and humid, such as rain forests, have complex food webs and a rich variety of species. Producers in a rain forest include mosses, ferns, wildflowers, grasses, vines, shrubs, and trees. Primary consumers include toucans, iguanas, and monkeys that eat fruit from the trees. Secondary consumers include hawks, boa

The ring-tailed lemur is a primary consumer in Madagascar that feeds on fruit and eggs. The lemurs also act as secondary consumers, feeding on birds, insects, and other small animals.

**DID YOU KNOW?**

In areas of New Guinea and Indonesia, there is a species of spiders known as bird-catching spiders. These spiders can build webs up to 3 feet (1 m) in diameter that can ensnare reptiles and small birds.

constrictors, and jaguars that eat the monkeys.

In contrast, Arctic food webs are much less complex. Because of the low temperatures, icy winds, and soil that stays frozen much of the year, plant growth is limited. Many plants are stunted or have a very short growing season. This limits the number and variety of consumers. The top predators may not be large animals, and they might be only at the secondary consumer trophic level.

## LIFE WITHOUT LIGHT

A unique food web exists in an area where life was once considered impossible—on the deep sea floor. Scientists once believed that all life forms depended on the sun for energy. But in 1977, scientists discovered hot springs on the ocean floor near South America that support life.

The springs—called hydrothermal vents or smokers—were far deeper than the sun's rays could penetrate. Yet entire

animal communities thrived around them. Noxious hydrogen sulfide gas spewed from the vents, but clams, fish, crabs, and giant tubeworms all lived nearby.

Certain types of bacteria live in the body cavities of some of these animals. The bacteria use sulfur-containing molecules—instead of sunlight—to produce nutrients. This process is called chemosynthesis. Rather than being poisoned by the hydrogen sulfide gas, the bacteria use it to create

The hydrogen sulfide gas billowing from a hydrothermal vent comes from volcanic fluid in Earth's crust that can reach 680 F (360 C).

carbohydrates. These nutrients move into the bodies of the host animals, providing a food supply. Giant tubeworms, for example, have no mouth, no stomach, and no digestive tract. Instead, their bodies are loaded with sulfide-using bacteria that provide the worms' food.

Tubeworms are among the few species that can survive in the deepest areas of the ocean.

Clearly, food webs exist in a great variety of places. As scientists continue to explore different environments, they discover new species and new food web relationships. Places that once were thought to be hostile to life—the driest regions of deserts, the deepest parts of the ocean, and the darkest of caves—have been found to have intricate and complex food webs.

Regardless of where food webs are found, it is important to study and understand them. Only by knowing the relationships within food webs will we be able to protect the plants and animals that form them.

Predators such as piranhas exist in numerous food webs around the world.

autotrophs—organisms that can make their own food by using materials in their environment

biological magnification—process by which toxic materials become more concentrated in animals at higher trophic levels

carnivores—meat-eaters

chemosynthesis—production of nutrients by autotrophs using chemical energy rather than solar energy

consumers—organisms in a food web that eat plants or animals

decomposers—organisms, usually bacteria or fungi, that break down dead plants and animals into simpler substances

food chain—series of organisms in which each one in the series eats the one preceding it

food web—multiple food chains connected within an ecosystem

herbivores—plant-eaters

heterotrophs—organisms that cannot make their own food and must eat other organisms

invasive species—plant or animal that has been artificially introduced into an ecosystem

limiting factor—living or nonliving entity whose supply in the environment limits the population of a species

omnivores—species that eat both plants and animals

trophic levels—levels of a food chain or food web

▷ Some top predators have unusual ways of obtaining their food. The bald eagle, for example, preys on fish, small mammals, and other birds. It also steals food from the osprey, a bird that excels at catching fish. Because of this habit, Benjamin Franklin considered the eagle to be "immoral" and voted against it becoming a symbol of the United States.

▷ Decomposers can release a significant amount of heat as they break down plant materials. Some people are trying to capture and use that heat. They are creating compost piles with built-in water pipes. Water runs through the pipes and heats up. Then the water is pumped into a nearby home.

▷ Many consumers change their feeding habits as they age. Larval fish, for example, usually feed on zooplankton and phytoplankton. However, as adults, they may eat plankton, decaying material on the bottom of a lake, or other fish.

▷ According to the National Invasive Species Information Center, invading organisms cause considerable environmental damage. For example, emerald ash borers are beetles that came to the United States in wood shipped from Asia. Young borers eat the inner bark of ash trees, slowly killing them. They have destroyed millions of trees in Michigan, Ohio, and Indiana. The center estimates the cost of such damage by invaders at around $120 billion each year.

▷ People think of herbivores as small animals, and they think of predators and carnivores as large animals. However, the African elephant—the largest land animal today—is a plant eater. It spends most of its day finding and eating grasses, leaves, twigs, bark, fruit, or flowers.

An African elephant can weigh up to 6 tons (5.4 metric tons). A single African elephant can consume up to 300 pounds (135 kg) of plants and 40 gallons (152 liters) of water a day.

## Further Reading

Griswell, Kim T. *Carnivorous Plants*. San Diego: KidHaven Press, 2003.

Lynch, Emma. *Ocean Food Chains*. Chicago: Heinemann Library, 2005.

Spilsbury, Louise, and Richard Spilsbury. *Desert Food Chains*. Chicago: Heinemann Library, 2005.

Wallace, Holly. *Food Chains and Webs*. Chicago: Heinemann Library, 2006.

## On the Web

For more information on this subject, use Facthound.
1. Go to *www.facthound.com*
2. Type in this book ID: 0756532612
3. Click on the Fetch It button.
Facthound will find the best Web sites for you.

## On the Road

**Milstein Hall of Ocean Life**
American Museum of Natural History
Central Park West and 79th Street
New York, NY 10024-5192
212/769-5100

**Messages From the Wilderness**
The Field Museum
1400 S. Lake Shore Drive
Chicago, IL 60605-2496
312/922-9410

## Explore all the Life Science books

Animal Cells: The Smallest Units of Life

DNA: The Master Molecule of Life

Food Webs: Interconnecting Food Chains

Genetics: A Living Blueprint

Human Body Systems: Maintaining the Body's Functions

Major Organs: Sustaining Life

Plant Cells: The Building Blocks of Plants

A complete list of Exploring Science titles is available on our Web site: *www.compasspointbooks.com*